DRUGS the facts about
AMPHETAMINES

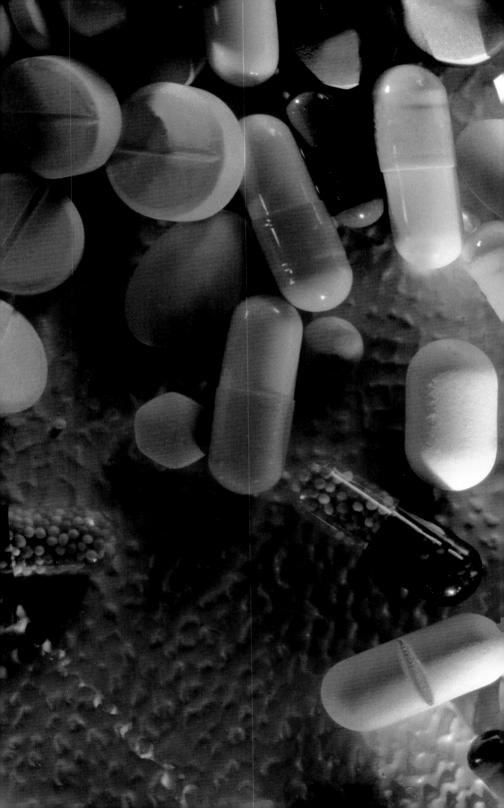

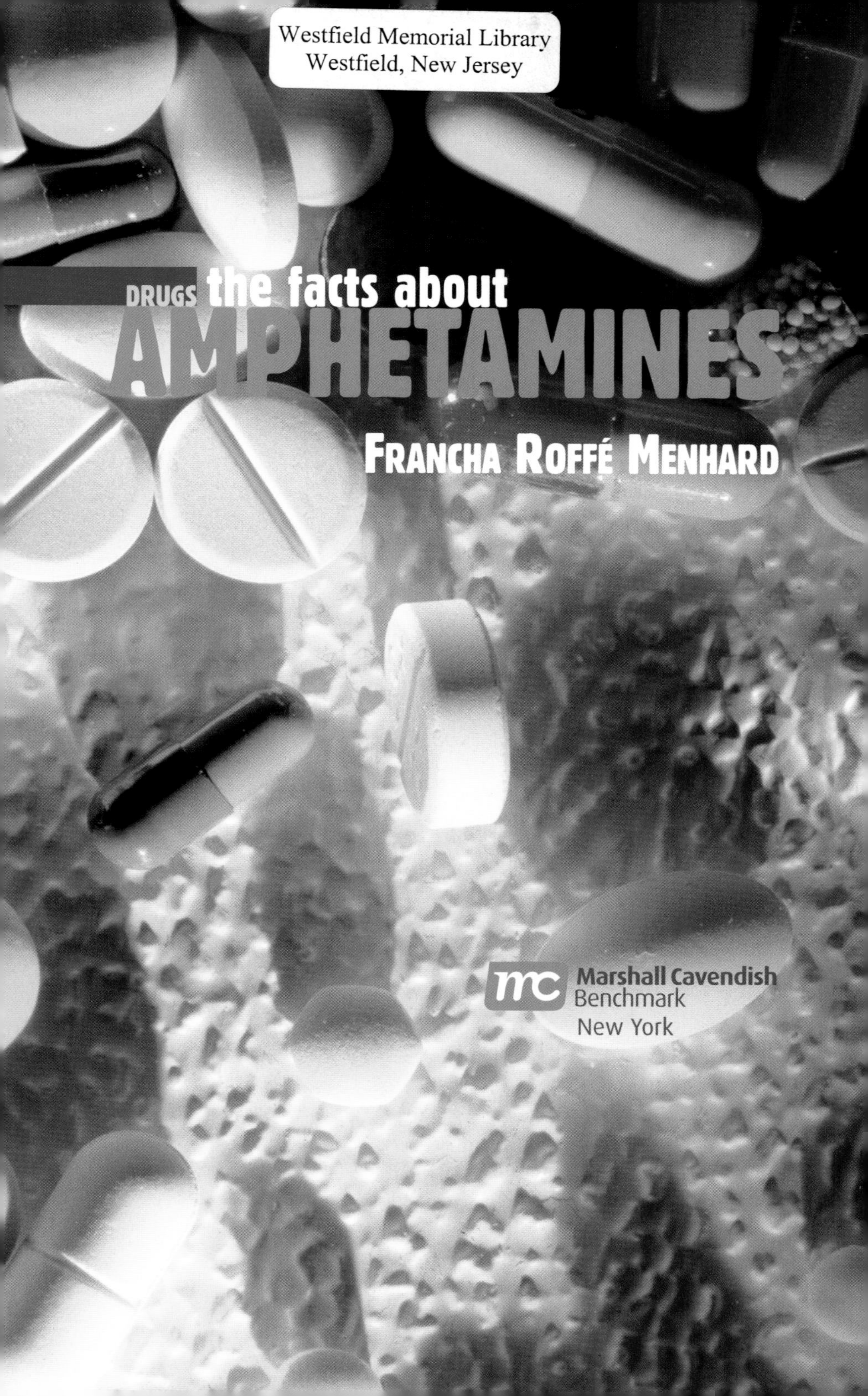

DRUGS the facts about
AMPHETAMINES

Francha Roffé Menhard

mc **Marshall Cavendish**
Benchmark
New York

Series Consultant: Dr. Amy Kohn, Chief Executive Officer, YWCA of
White Plains and Central Westchester, New York.
Thanks to John M. Roll, Ph.D., Director of Behavioral Pharmacology at UCLA Integrated
Substance Abuse Programs, for his expert reading of this manuscript.

Marshall Cavendish Benchmark
99 White Plains Road
Tarrytown, New York 10591
www.marshallcavendish.us

For Nick, who always says, "You can do this."

Library of Congress Cataloging-in-Publication Data

Menhard, Francha Roffé.
The facts about amphetamines / by Francha Roffé Menhard.— 1st ed.
p. cm. — (Drugs)
Summary: "Describes the history, characteristics, legal status, and abuse
of amphetamines and methamphetamines"—Provided by publisher.
Includes bibliographical references and index.
ISBN 0-7614-1972-1
1. Amphetamine abuse—Juvenile literature. 2. Methamphetamine
abuse—Juvenile literature. 3. Amphetamines—Juvenile literature. I.
Title. II. Series: Drugs (Benchmark Books (Firm))

RC568.A45M46 2005
362.29'9—dc22
2005001142

Photo Research by Joan Meisel

Cover photo: Royalty-Free/Corbis

The photographs in this book are used by permission and through the courtesy of:
AP/Wide World: 56, 59, 66. Alamy: 22. Peter Arnold, Inc.: D. Hurst, 40. Corbis: 1, 2-3, 5;
Royalty-Free, 24; Bettmann, 28, 31, 32. Getty
Images: Time Life Pictures, 15. Photo Researchers, Inc.: Tek Image, 8; Bluestone, 26.

Printed in China

1 3 5 6 4 2

CONTENTS

INTRODUCTION

THEY ARE CHEAP. They are easy to get. They make people feel good, strong, confident, and energized. They have longer lasting effects than cocaine. They are a group of stimulants called amphetamines. Amphetamines cause a cocaine-like rush that mimics the body's natural adrenaline. Amphetamines energize the brain. They increase heart rate, blood pressure, and breathing.

At first, amphetamines can make the user feel invigorated. Users describe it as feeling that, "I'm good enough, handsome enough, and smart enough." Insecurities and self-doubt disappear.

But then it takes more and more of the drug to create the same good feeling, so users take more and more—more and more often. The user experiences an ever-decreasing high, as amphetamines drain the brain of necessary chemicals. Many experience paranoia and physical degeneration, and exhibit violent behavior.

Amphetamines quickly become the user's worst enemy. They cause skin eruptions, which are something like acne. Some users think they see bugs crawling on their skin. They scratch themselves until they bleed. They feel confused and anxious. They cannot sleep. "Write all your dreams on a piece of paper," says one high school girl. "Now tear up the paper and throw it in the trash. That's what happens when you take amphetamines."

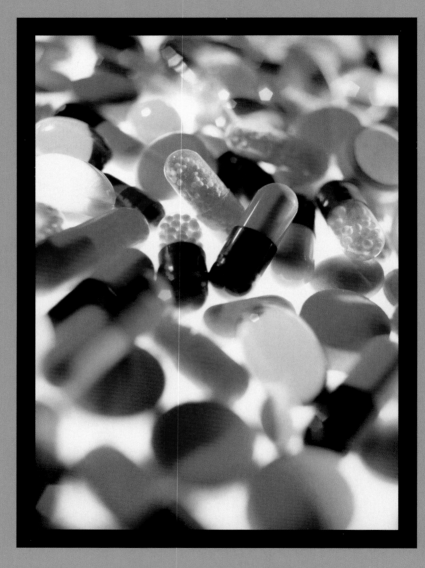

AMPHETAMINES ARE POWERFUL STIMULANTS THAT ARE OFTEN PRESCRIBED TO COMBAT FATIGUE, OBESITY, AND ATTENTION DEFICIT DISORDERS.

1 What Are Amphetamines?

AMPHETAMINES are a group of synthetic, or artificial, drugs commonly called speed or uppers. They are stimulants, which means they increase the action of the central nervous system (brain and spinal cord). They kick the body into emergency mode and release the body's natural adrenaline in high amounts.

The chemical structure of amphetamine is similar to that of ephedrine, which occurs naturally in the plant species *Ephedraceae*. Over forty species of *Ephedraceae* are found throughout Asia, Europe, the Mediterranean, and in North and South America. Ephedrine was used for thousands of years in China to treat asthma. Ephedra, a derivative of *Ephedraceae*, was used until recently for weight loss, as an energy booster, and to enhance athletic performance.

Baseball's Dirty Little Secret

Athletes use a number of illicit substances in order to enhance performance. Although amphetamines do increase a person's confidence and aggression they do not improve athletic performance. Amphetamines cause impaired judgment, which can lead one to participate in activities while injured. This could lead to worse injury or risk to other players. Using amphetamines during physical activity can also lead to heatstroke. While amphetamine use by athletes is not as widespread as steroid use, it is still a serious problem in professional as well as youth sports.

The use of amphetamines by major league baseball players has been called baseball's "dirty little secret." The secret was exposed by former major-league outfielder Chad Curtis in an interview in May 2005. In the wake of major scandals concerning use of steroids in baseball, Curtis told reporter Armen Keteyian that he believed about 20 percent of big-leaguers used steroids, and 85 percent have taken "an illegal substance for energy." The use of amphetamines is banned by the NFL, NBA, and the International Olympic Committee but not by Major League Baseball. The investigation into their use may well change that.

Amphetamines are prescribed for people with fatigue, depression, obesity, attention deficit disorders, and narcolepsy, which is a disease that makes people suddenly fall into a deep sleep. Some amphetamines are available over the counter at drugstores in decongestants and some diet pills.

Amphetamine-containing diet pills, such as Dexatrim and Acutrim, became available over the counter in 1979. People bought them by the millions. These drugs suppressed appetite and gastrointestinal activity and accelerated the body's metabolism. The downside was that as time went on, dieters needed higher and higher doses to keep losing weight. Dependency was a definite risk.

Appetite suppressants also had unpleasant side effects. They caused increased heart rate and irregular heartbeat, rise in blood pressure, dry mouth, and blurred vision. Some dieters experienced lightheadedness, hallucinations, paranoia, and addiction. In 1989 alone, the American Association of Poison Control Centers received 47,000 complaints related to these drugs.

Adderall and Ritalin

More than 80 percent of prescription amphetamine use in the United States is for treatment of attention deficit disorders (ADD), according to the Drug Enforcement Agency (DEA). Adderall, a close chemical cousin of Dexedrine, is the most commonly prescribed. It is also the most commonly abused prescription amphetamine.

The amphetamine mix now called Adderall dates back to 1960. At that time, Rexar Pharmaceuticals called it Obetrol and marketed it for obesity. Adderall joined the already soaring market for drugs to treat Attention Deficit Hyperactivity Disorder (ADHD), and, almost immediately, sales of the drug skyrocketed. By the end of 1999, Adderall accounted for 28 percent of ADHD drug sales in the United States.

Although many children take these drugs every day with no problems, others experience disturbing side effects, including changes in sleep patterns and abnormalities in brain development. They also have a high likelihood of abuse and dependence.

Adderall as a drug of abuse is not primarily a party drug. Most of those who use the drug without a prescription just want to be able to concentrate and feel more alert and energetic in order to keep up with their busy schedules. Some believe they have undiagnosed ADHD and need the drug to succeed in school. Even college students— one in five reports using such drugs without a prescription—buy, sell, or steal prescription ADHD drugs.

Ritalin (methylphenidate) is a mild nervous system stimulant and is similar to amphetamine-based ADHD drugs. Like amphetamines, its stimulant effects include appetite suppression, sleeplessness, increased attentiveness and focus, and euphoria.

Mark is a college student who uses Adderall. The junior has used the drug since final exam week when he was a freshman, and he is sure he would never have passed chemistry without it. He buys the drug for three or four dollars from a student who has a prescription but does not need it any more. "I'll take half a pill and study for two or three hours, and remember everything," Mark says. "It keeps you focused on the one thing you're trying to learn." That their peers use amphetamines to study makes other students mad. "Performance-enhancing drugs are not acceptable in athletics," said one University of Chicago student. "They shouldn't be acceptable in academics either."

Ritalin has been around since the 1950s but it only became common in the late 1980s. Today, doctors write some 9 million prescriptions for Ritalin each year.

With that much Ritalin available, abuse is not uncommon. Some users "stack" the drug Ecstasy with Ritalin so that their high will last longer, but most use so-called "Vitamin R" or the "Smart Drug" to study and concentrate in school. In fact, almost 7 percent of high school students had used Ritalin illegally in 1996, according to a 1997 Indiana University study, and some 2.5 percent had used it monthly or more often. Data from the 2003 Monitoring the Future study, which is funded annually by the National Institute on Drug Abuse (NIDA), show 2.6

percent of eighth graders, 4.1 percent of tenth graders, and 4.0 percent of twelfth graders having abused Ritalin.

Many teens do not consider illegal abuse of Ritalin to be serious. After all, if six-year-olds take it, how harmful can it be? The truth is that the effects of Ritalin abuse are similar to those of cocaine. Like other ADHD drugs, Ritalin can cause abnormalities in brain development and sleep patterns, as well as psychosis and, rarely, death.

Methamphetamine

Methamphetamine is a type of amphetamine. It is the most commonly abused form of amphetamine and is highly addictive. Methamphetamine is legally available by prescription and is sometimes pre-scribed for attention deficit disorders and certain types of obesity. It is also available without prescrip-tion in nasal decongestants.

There are two types of illegal methampheta-mine. Dextro-levo-methamphetamine has been illegally produced in the United States since the late 1970s. Production and use of this type is limited. The other, more potent type is dextro-metham-phetamine. This highly addictive substance is the most widely abused type of amphetamine.

Illegal methamphetamine comes in three forms—powder, crystal, and tablets. The most common in the United States is powdered methamphetamine, also called crystal meth or

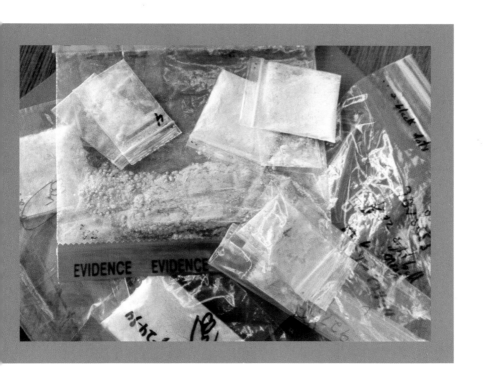

THESE PLASTIC BAGS OF METHAMPHETAMINE WERE SEIZED IN A DRUG RAID IN BILLINGS, MONTANA.

crank. "Meth cooks" produce the crystalline, bitter-tasting, water-soluble drug in small home laboratories. Powdered meth comes in several colors—white, pink, red, tan, and brown—depending what other chemicals are used to produce it. The powder is generally snorted or injected, but some swallow or smoke it.

Crystal or ice methamphetamine, also called glass, shabu, or batu, gets its name from its

Common Street Names for Amphetamines

Amphetamines (includes Methamphetamines):
Pink hearts
Speed
White cross

Methamphetamine:
Bathtub crank (poor quality, sometimes produced in bathtubs)
Black beauty
Blue meth
Crank
Crystal meth
Geep
Lemon drop (has a dull yellow tint)
Meth
Rock
Scootie
Sketch
Sparkle
Speckled birds
Spoosh
Tina
Trash
Wash

Working man's cocaine
Yellow bam
Yellow powder

Smokable Methamphetamine:
Batu
Cristy
Hanyak
Hironpon
Hiropon
Hot ice
Kaksonjae
L.A. glass
L.A. ice
Quartz
Super ice

Crystal Methamphetamine:
Blade
Crypto
Crystal
Crystal glass
Ice
Stove top

appearance; it looks like rock candy or shards of ice. Crystal meth is a pure, highly addictive form of methamphetamine. Cooks recrystallize powdered methamphetamine in a solvent such as water, methanol, ethanol, isopropanol, or acetone to remove its impurities. Users typically smoke crystal meth.

Methamphetamine tablets generally contain a combination of powdered methamphetamine and caffeine. Most tablets are either green or orange-red, and some are designed to smell and taste like candy. The tablets can be swallowed, but some users melt it and sniff the vapors. Crushed tablets are snorted or mixed with a solvent and injected.

Who Uses Amphetamines?

Amphetamine abusers are usually between twelve and twenty-five years of age. They frequently find themselves in situations that encourage drug abuse, and they are likely to experience peer pressure to use amphetamines. Children whose parents are dependent on mood-altering drugs may be more likely to try them.

It is difficult to know how many Americans use amphetamines, but Aegis Sciences Corporation, a federally certified forensic toxicology laboratory that does drug screening tests, estimates that 13 million Americans use amphetamines illegally.

Trends in Annual Use, Risk, of Amphetamines

Use
% who used in last twelve months

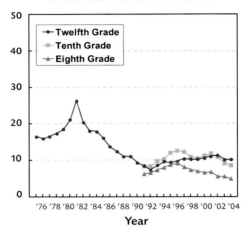

Risk
% seeing "great risk" in using once or twice

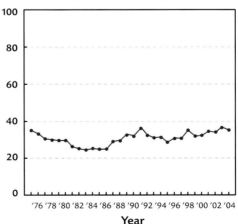

Disapproval
% disapproving of using once or twice

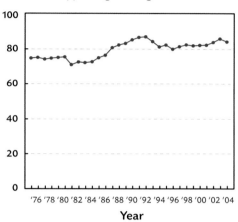

Year

Availability
% saying "fairly easy" or "very easy" to get

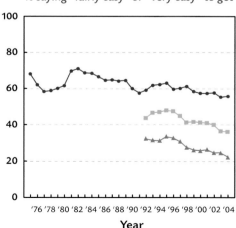

Year

SOURCE: 2004 MONITORING THE FUTURE STUDY

The 2004 Monitoring the Future study found that while use of amphetamines by eighth and tenth graders decreased significantly between 2000 and 2004, use among twelfth graders remained steady. Methamphetamine use has decreased in nearly all grades, with twelfth graders showing a slight increase between 2003 and 2004.

Approximately 1.5 million people used methamphetamine in 2001, according to the 2002 National Survey on Drug Use and Health (NSDUH). This is much lower than the number of people who used marijuana (approximately 25.7 million) and cocaine (approximately 7.4 million), but higher than the number of people who have used heroin (approximately 404,000).

Methamphetamine abusers are mostly white, lower middle income, high school educated, adult males between the ages of twenty and thirty-five, though use by women and members of other ethnic groups is growing. Most begin snorting methamphetamine and progress to smoking or injecting the drug. The typical person who makes and provides meth to others is an unemployed white male between fifteen and thirty years old, poor and poorly educated.

In 2003, when the use of other drugs in the adult workplace was dropping, use of amphetamine and methamphetamine was on the rise. Although most office workers who abused stimulants continued to prefer cocaine, use of amphetamines rose 17 percent in 2002 and was up 70 percent since 1997.

Of every 10,000 workers, thirty-four tested positive in 2002, up from twenty-nine in 2001 and twenty in 1998. And, about 1.2 percent of fourth-year medical students reported using amphetamines.

THE EPHEDRACEAE PLANT CONTAINS THE HERBAL STIMULANT EPHEDRINE, WHICH WAS USED FOR YEARS IN OVER-THE-COUNTER REMEDIES FOR OBESITY AND FATIGUE. IN 2004, THE FDA BANNED EPHEDRINE FOR USE IN EVERYTHING EXCEPT PRESCRIPTION MEDICATIONS.

2 A History of Speed

A SPECIES OF the *Ephedraceae* plant, which contains the herbal stimulant ephedrine, was found in a Neanderthal grave from the Middle Paleolithic period (20,000 years ago) in what is now Iraq. It is thought that it was probably used as a medicine. The first written record of the use of a natural amphetamine appears in a Chinese herbal book written nearly 5,000 years ago. Dioscorides, the famous Greek physician, documented using ephedra in 80 C.E.

The species known as *Ma Huang* in China is an almost leafless evergreen shrub that grows between 2 and 3 feet (about 1 meter) high. Known as ephedra in the West, its slender, erect stems are green, small-ribbed, and sharp-pointed with small triangular leaves at the stem nodes. The nodes are generally reddish brown. The plant has a very harsh taste and yellowish leaves. The Chinese word *Ma* means astringent or bitter, and *Huang* means yellow, though some say that *Ma Huang* can be translated as "asking for trouble."

Chinese herbalists sun-dried the stems of *Ma Huang* and ground them for use in tea. The tea was used for colds, flu, fever, chills, headache, edema, bronchial asthma, nasal congestion, aching joints and bones, coughs, wheezing, allergies, bronchial congestion, low blood pressure, and hives. They also used ephedra to force people with fevers to perspire and to control night sweats. Chinese armies used *Ma Huang* to prevent fatigue and improve stamina during wartime.

CHINESE DOCTORS STARTED USING EPHEDRINE TO TREAT A NUMBER OF COMPLAINTS, SUCH AS COLDS, FLU, HEADACHE, AND NASAL CONGESTION, NEARLY 5,000 YEARS AGO.

Native Americans prepared leaves and stems from an ephedra-containing plant in a tea for stomach and bowel disorders, for colds, fever, and headache. They made poultices from dried, powdered twigs for burns and ointments for sores. One tribe used the entire plant in a tea and drank it to help stop bleeding. Mormon pioneers, whose religion did not permit drinking tea or coffee, used ephedra plants to make a hot drink, sweetened with sugar or strawberry jam, that was given several names, including Mormon tea, Brigham tea, Desert tea, and Teamster's tea. Some settlers drank the bitter-tasting tea as a cure for syphilis and gonorrhea, although there was no proof it actually worked.

In 1887, German chemist L. Edeleano first synthesized amphetamine and named it phenylisopropylamine. Japanese chemist A. Ogata synthesized methamphetamine, stronger and easier to make than amphetamine, in 1919. Crystalline methamphetamine powder was soluble in water, making it easy to prepare for injection.

In the 1920s, military organizations throughout the world realized that the anti-fatigue properties of amphetamines could be useful on the battlefield. The United States military conducted extensive tests of caffeine pills but high doses of caffeine caused soldiers' hands to shake and interfered with aiming weapons.

Around the same time, amphetamines were tested on humans as a cure or treatment against a

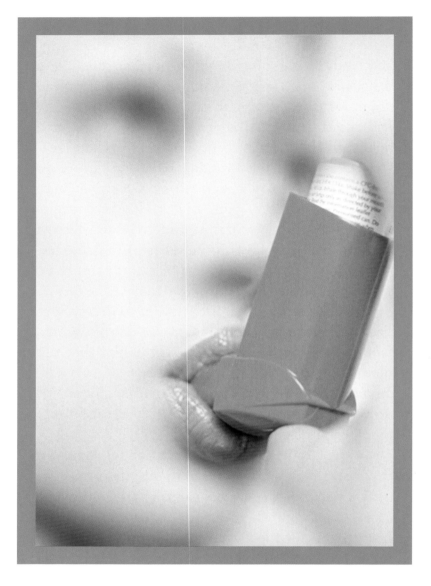

AMPHETAMINES HAVE BEEN USED TO TREAT BRONCHIAL ASTHMA SINCE THE 1920S.

variety of illnesses and maladies, including epilepsy, schizophrenia, alcoholism, opiate addiction, migraine, head injuries, and irradiation sickness among many others. Amphetamine proved of use in people with asthma and other respiratory ailments.

In 1927, a University of California researcher, Gordon Alles, synthesized a new form of amphetamine, which he called Benzedrine. An over-the-counter inhaler was made available for those suffering with nasal or bronchial congestion due to asthma, allergies, and colds. Physicians then found that amphetamine was useful in treating narcolepsy, a disease characterized by brief attacks of deep sleep that can occur at any time without warning.

College students discovered that amphetamines could help them stay awake to study for exams. Businessmen and secretaries found the drug helped them overcome fatigue. It also helped long-haul truck drivers stay awake on the road so they could drive longer and make more money. Athletes found that amphetamines increased their alertness and energy level.

In 1937, researchers confirmed that amphetamines helped some children with Attention Deficit Disorder (ADD) to concentrate. The same year, amphetamine was introduced in prescription tablet form for use as a weight-loss drug. Nicknamed speed, Benzedrine became popular among recreational drug users. Its effects were similar to cocaine.

ADOLF HITLER RECEIVED DAILY AMPHETAMINE INJECTIONS FROM HIS PERSONAL PHYSICIAN, THEODORE MORRELL.

The high was not quite as intense, but lasted longer. And, unlike cocaine, Benzedrine was legal.

Amphetamines in Wartime

As Germany moved toward war, Adolf Hitler, whose doctor injected him with amphetamine daily, encouraged those close to him to take it, too. He also ordered that his soldiers be supplied with amphetamines and between April and December 1939 German troops received some 29 million Pervitine pills.

During World War II, Canadian, U.S., and Japanese soldiers were issued amphetamine pills to help them stay alert and to reduce fatigue. German Luftwaffe crews on long-range flights used amphetamines. However, the German high command was disturbed by the drug's side effects, and amphetamines were prohibited after Russians captured a company of elite Waffen SS troops who had guns but no ammunition. In a fit of paranoia after heavy amphetamine use, the men had wasted all their ammunition firing at imaginary enemies the night before.

Japan supplied amphetamines not only to soldiers but also to industrial workers on the home front. During the American occupation of Japan after the war, citizens of the defeated nation turned for comfort to amphetamines that the government had stockpiled.

It is widely thought that U.S. soldiers, sailors, and pilots consumed over 200 million amphetamine pills during World War II. Some soldiers report that they borrowed the drug from the British. Others say that medics distributed it unofficially. Pilots have reported that their survival kits included the drug in candy form. Rumors spread that C-Rations laced with the drug were issued to General Patton's troops during the Battle of the Bulge.

On the American home front, truck stops sold amphetamines alongside coffee and caffeine tablets. Students used so-called pep pills to help them stay awake to cram for exams. By 1948, two-thirds of weight-loss patients were taking amphetamine-based prescription drugs. But at this time, though enormous quantities of oral amphetamines were being consumed, there was apparently little misuse or abuse.

After World War II, some troubled veterans went home to join motorcycle gangs. Many continued taking amphetamines. Some graduated from taking pills to injecting intravenously. When they could no longer find legal amphetamine, they learned to make methamphetamine on their own. Riders often hid it in the crank case of their bikes and began to call the drug crank.

During the Korean War (1950-1953), methamphetamine was made available to U.S. forces in order to fight off massive waves of Chinese infantry assaults that often lasted late into the night. In Korea and Japan in the early 1950s, servicemen first injected amphetamines intravenously. Some mixed heroin with amphetamine and brought the habit home with them at the end of their tour of duty.

Increase in Recreational Use

Legally manufactured tablets of both dextroamphetamine (Dexedrine) and methamphetamine

THIS **1960** PHOTOGRAPH SHOWS POLICE DETECTIVES POURING **15,000** AMPHETAMINE PILLS INTO AN INCINERATOR. THE PILLS WERE CONFISCATED FROM GAS STATION ATTENDANTS WHO WERE SELLING THEM TO TRUCKERS.

(Methedrine) became readily available around 1950. They were used for performance enhancement by college students, truck drivers, and athletes. By the early 1960s, amphetamines were popular on the street. Injectable methamphetamine became widely available as well.

In 1962, the government cracked down on doctors and pharmacists who were selling prescriptions for injectable amphetamine. A nationwide media campaign warned of the dangers of intravenous amphetamine use.

The American Medical Association's Council on Drugs admitted that people might be abusing amphetamines, but reported that compulsive abuse constituted only a small problem. That same year, however, most major pharmaceutical companies withdrew injectable amphetamine ampoules from the market. Illegal laboratories sprang up as legal amphetamines disappeared from pharmacies. By the end of 1963, there were several highly profitable illegal labs in San Francisco supplying amphetamines to drug users.

During the Vietnam War, use of methamphetamine was widespread. In fact, during that war

THE U.S. NAVY AND AIR FORCE GAVE AMPHETAMINES TO PILOTS DURING THE VIETNAM WAR. STIMULANTS, NICKNAMED GO-PILLS, WERE ALTERNATED WITH TRANQUILIZERS, OR NO-GO PILLS, BY FLIGHT SURGEONS TO MANAGE FATIGUE AND MAINTAIN PILOT PERFORMANCE. IT IS BELIEVED THAT THESE ARE STILL ADMINISTERED TODAY BY MILITARY FLIGHT SURGEONS.

American soldiers used more amphetamines than soldiers on both sides had used during World War II. Nocturnal mortar attacks and the fatigue that followed meant that soldiers continued to take methamphetamine. The official army prescription called for one 2-milligram tablet of dextroamphetamine when "readiness is required with 48 hours of no sleep."

But according to a study involving urinalysis of U.S. Army enlistees returning home, addiction and use of amphetamines, barbiturates, and opiates was less a problem than many people had expected. Of the 13,760 men tested, some 1,400—about 10 percent—tested positive for amphetamines, barbiturates, or opiates. A year later, 92 percent of the original group were drug-free. Even as troops were issued amphetamines, Congress passed the U.S. Drug Abuse Regulation and Control Act of 1970, which restricted legal access to amphetamines. This led to a black market in amphetamines and a proliferation of underground laboratories.

Smokable methamphetamines—called crystal meth or ice—appeared in the early 1980s. Ice is a highly purified form of crystal that looks like a crystal rock. Methamphetamine use was largely a problem in the western United States. In 1981, the federal Drug Enforcement Agency (DEA) seized 184 underground labs across the United States. In 1989, they seized over eight hundred labs.

By the early nineties, Americans were beginning to realize how dangerous amphetamine could be.

Even so, some soldiers serving in the first Gulf War (1991) took pills issued by the U.S. military. Air Force guidelines during that war called for the distribution of six 5-milligram tablets with all pilots closely monitored by a flight surgeon.

During the 1990s, organized crime syndicates operating out of Mexico replaced the outlaw motorcycle gangs that had dominated methamphetamine trafficking in the U.S. for twenty years. Using their well-established marijuana, cocaine, and heroin distribution networks, they moved unprecedented amounts of highly pure meth across the United States.

In 1997, methamphetamine began to emerge as a drug of choice in the West, Southwest, and the South, then spread into rural areas across the United States. The production of methamphetamine moved from drug corporations to clandestine laboratories in hotel rooms, cars, and kitchens, as well as huge laboratories in Mexico and California.

Between 2000 and 2002, law enforcement seized several bulk shipments of pseudoephedrine, which is one of the materials, or precursor chemicals, used to manufacture meth. Pseudoephedrine is used in the manufacture of some over-the-counter decongestants. The involvement of organized crime drug groups in these shipments focused attention on the need to cut off supplies of pseudoephedrine and other such chemicals. New laws were instituted to control manufacture and distribution of precursor chemicals. These laws led to a decrease in availability of amphetamine. This, in turn, increased the

Myths about Amphetamines

MYTH: It is possible to use amphetamines recreationally, limiting use to once or twice a month.

The facts: It is extremely rare for people to be able to control amphetamine abuse. One of the characteristics of amphetamines is that they change the brain in such a way that users get hooked quickly and need more and more of the drug to keep from experiencing painful withdrawal.

MYTH: Amphetamine abuse is an urban problem.

The facts: Meth is every bit as much a problem in rural areas as in cities, if not more so. Rural areas, with their network of narrow roads and sparse populations, are ideal places to hide illegal labs. Economically depressed areas have long been centers for illicit drug use, and the supplies needed to manufacture meth are inexpensive and easy to find.

MYTH: Meth addiction is untreatable.

The facts: Addiction to methamphetamine is difficult to treat. During withdrawal, former users experience a devastating inability to experience pleasure. The desperate attempt to recreate the intense pleasure that meth created at first often causes relapse. Still, treatment programs for meth addiction have approximately the same success as those for cocaine. About 50 to 60 percent of patients remain drug-free after one year.

price of illegal amphetamines. In Washington State in particular, the price increase caused some meth users to switch to cocaine.

Meth in the Heartland

The illegal manufacture and use of methamphetamine is a serious law enforcement problem in rural America. While most other illicit drug use is centered in cities, meth is a problem in smaller towns and rural areas, with the exception of crystal meth, which is more common in large cities.

Eighth graders in rural areas are twice as likely to have used amphetamines in the past month than eighth graders in urban areas, the National Center on Addiction and Substance Abuse at Columbia University reported in 2000. In cities with populations smaller than 10,000, drug arrests increased six times as fast as those in cities with populations of 250,000 or larger.

Meth is also more likely to be manufactured in the rural United States than imported from Mexico's laboratories. No sophisticated equipment is required, and the ingredients are easy to acquire. Meth cooks whip up batches of the drug in barns and shacks across rural America. Anhydrous ammonia, a substance used in making meth, is used as fertilizer and is therefore available in these areas in large quantities.

Meth cooks generally do not make the drug for profit. They do what they do largely to feed their own addiction. Coming from depressed areas with

DEA Meth Lab Seizures

THESE MAPS SHOW ALL METH-RELATED INCIDENTS REPORTED BY THE **DEA** IN **1999** AND IN **2004**. NOTE THAT THE HIGHEST RATE OF INCIDENCE HAS MOVED FROM THE **WEST COAST**, WHERE **CALIFORNIA** HAD **2,579** INCIDENTS IN **1999**, TO THE **MIDWEST**, WITH **2,786** INCIDENTS IN **MISSOURI** IN **2004**.

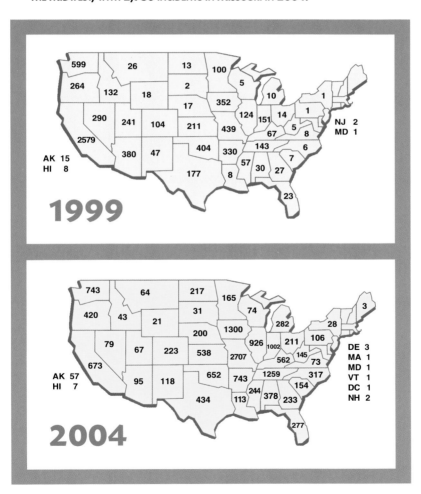

> Anhydrous ammonia thieves had better beware. Farmers can add a new product, GloTell, to their tanks. Meth cooks will run the risk that the additive will turn their hands bright pink—a stain that, even if washed off, will fluoresce under ultraviolet light. It will also produce pink methamphetamine that cannot be bleached. Users who snort meth made with GloTell will find that they have pink noses. Those who inject the drug will see a pink stain at the point of injection.

few jobs, they use the drug in an attempt to escape their hard lives.

Although methamphetamine use is an epidemic across the U.S., the problem has grown most drastically in the Midwest. Meth accounts for nearly 90 percent of all drug cases in the midwestern states. As the taste for meth has grown, hundreds of small, clandestine "mom-and-pop" labs have sprung up to cook less than an ounce of meth at a time. In California, the number of clandestine lab seizures has dropped dramatically with aggressive control of the chemicals required to cook meth. That does not mean that methamphetamine is not still a problem in California. More and more, according to the DEA, meth in California comes from labs in Mexico, where precursor chemicals are easy to acquire.

As long as amphetamines are available, teens and adults will continue to experiment with them and become addicted. Some will recover, but some will destroy their lives permanently. Law enforcement will continue to search for and destroy meth labs. And governments will continue to debate the issue of how to best deal with the problem.

A LAW ENFORCEMENT OFFICIAL IN A PROTECTIVE SUIT CARRIES A BOX OF TOXIC SUPPLIES OUT OF A METH LAB IN POLK COUNTY, OREGON. THE MANUFACTURE OF METHAMPHETAMINE HAS A SEVERE IMPACT ON THE ENVIRONMENT. THE PRODUCTION OF ONE POUND (.5 KILOGRAM) OF METHAMPHETAMINE RELEASES POISONOUS GAS INTO THE ATMOSPHERE AND CREATES 5 TO 7 (2.5-3 KILOGRAMS) POUNDS OF TOXIC WASTE.

3 The Dangers of Abuse

WHEN SAM STARTED using in high school, crystal meth reduced her feelings of depression and helped her lose weight. It did not take long, however, for her to start fighting with her parents and isolating herself from her friends who did not use drugs. She hid in her room, afraid that the police would come after her. She looked like a skeleton and her hair was falling out. She could not sleep.

Teens like Sam find it easy to ignore these costs when they first experiment with amphetamines. They do not realize that this drug exacts a high price—from their health, from their social life, from their community.

Innocent Children

Amphetamine abuse can harm unborn babies. Mothers who have used amphetamines may experience complications before, during, and after delivery. So-called amphetamine babies can suffer from developmental problems throughout their lives. They startle more easily and they grow up with lower inhibition, which can lead to lack of impulse control.

Rebecca Cole knows how hard it can be to deal with a baby who was exposed to amphetamines in the womb. In 2000, she and her husband adopted a five-month-old baby girl born to a mother who was addicted to methamphetamine. Little Natalie exhibited behaviors that shocked her new parents. Biting and head banging were just two of them. With intensive occupational and play therapy, Natalie was doing well by her third birthday—enjoying swimming and tumbling classes as well as preschool. But what if she had stayed with her meth-abusing mother?

Three-month-old Jacob Smith stayed with his mother, and she killed him with methamphetamine-tainted milk. Even when she found Jacob was not breathing, she did not call for help right away. Instead, she cleaned up the evidence of her meth lab first. A drug test showed that the mother had meth in her system. The baby may have died either because the mother was breast-feeding or because she put milk in a baby bottle liner that had been used to store the drug. Jacob's mother was convicted of murder and sentenced to life in prison.

In 2003, some 3,300 children were found living in meth labs, according to the DEA. Those children are exposed to the same chemicals as their meth-abusing parents.

ANDREA MOHIN/THE NEW YORK TIMES

A VOLUNTEER AT A SHELTER IN TULSA, OKLAHOMA, CUDDLES TWO CHILDREN WHO ARE AWAITING PLACEMENT IN FOSTER HOMES. MANY OF THE CHILDREN AT THIS SHELTER HAVE BEEN TAKEN FROM PARENTS WHO ABUSE METHAMPHETAMINES.

Long-term use of amphetamines leads to decreased sex drive and weight loss. People with high blood pressure or heart problems may damage blood vessels and risk heart failure. And intravenous methamphetamine users have a higher risk for contracting HIV/AIDS and hepatitis.

Amphetamine users also put others in danger. Their impulse control often causes them to become violent, emotionally and physically abusing the people around them. Their lack of judgment can lead to unnecessary accidents. Users who combine alcohol and amphetamines often commit unprovoked, random, and senseless acts of violence.

Socially, amphetamine abuse can lead to destruction of friendships and families. Amphetamine users lose interest in relationships that were once important to them. Many drop their non-using friends and spend time only with people who also use the drug. Young users often drop out of school. Family responsibilities and family members become less important than the drug.

Users may steal to get money for the drug—often from family members. They may lose their jobs or be arrested because of their drug use. Families may lose an income and plunge into poverty. Parents who take amphetamines are more likely to become violent with their children, and those who manufacture methamphetamine put their children in danger of poisoning, burns, and death. Children also suffer when a parent is jailed for possession or distribution.

Amphetamine addiction also puts a strain on the economic well being of the community. When an addict does not have private health insurance the community has to pick up the tab. Health costs of drug addicts are some 80 percent higher than those of non-addicts. Amphetamine use also leads to higher crime in communities, especially in the areas where organized gangs traffic methamphetamines.

How Amphetamines Affect the Brain

Snorted, smoked, or injected, amphetamine ends up in the bloodstream and is carried quickly to the brain. The brain is made up of billions of nerve cells, called neurons. Most neurons have three important parts:

- the **cell body** contains the nucleus and directs the activities of the neuron;
- **dendrites**, short fibers that receive messages from other neurons and relay them to the cell body;
- and an **axon**, one long single fiber that carries messages from the cell body to dendrites of other neurons.

The neuron sends a message to another neuron by releasing a chemical, called a neurotransmitter, from its axon into the small space that separates the two neurons. This space is called a synapse.

Protecting the Adolescent Brain

Drug use by adolescents can have devastating long-term consequences. Recent research shows that major changes take place in the brain during adolescence. A process called "pruning" of brain cells takes place during this time—certain brain cells are strengthened while weaker ones are eliminated. Using substances that interfere with the developing brain can negatively affect processes such as memory and attention. Many scientists believe that this damage is irreversible.

The neurotransmitter crosses the synapse and attaches to specific places on the dendrites of the neighboring neuron. These places are called receptors. Once the neurotransmitter has relayed its message, it is either used up or taken back up into the first neuron where it is recycled for future use. This process of recycling is called reuptake.

Amphetamines affect structures that contain a neurotransmitter called dopamine. Dopamine is sometimes called the pleasure neurotransmitter. When something good happens, certain axons release dopamine. The dopamine attaches to receptors on dendrites of neighboring neurons to transmit the pleasure message. Amphetamines interfere with this process.

Amphetamines fool the neurons, which take up

the drug as if it were actually dopamine. Once it gets inside a neuron, amphetamine tells the neuron to release large amounts dopamine. This large amount of dopamine produces a feeling of euphoria that can last all day. But after euphoria comes a "crash." Users feel depressed and exhausted. Amphetamine use leads to the destruction of brain cells containing dopamine, so the longer a person uses amphetamines the harder it is for them to experience normal feelings of pleasure and delight. The things that once made them feel happy no longer affect them.

How Amphetamines Affect the Body

Amphetamines affect the body in much the same way as the body's natural adrenaline. They make body systems run faster than normal. Amphetamine users are full of energy, contentment, and confidence for the first four to six hours after use. During this time, they will not feel hunger. Their hearts beat faster and their breathing speeds up. Their pupils widen. But amphetamines cannot create energy. The body uses energy it has stored up for tomorrow, next week, and next year.

Small doses increase respiration, heart rate, and blood pressure and dilate the pupils. Moderate doses can cause dry mouth, fever, sweating, headache, blurred vision, dizziness, diarrhea or constipation, and loss of appetite. Large doses can cause flushing, pallor, rapid and irregular heartbeat,

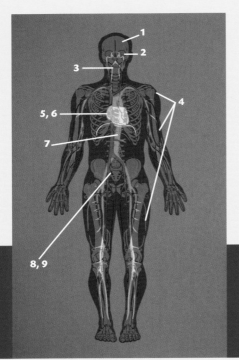

Effects of Amphetamines from Head to Toe

1 Change of mental status, disorientation, and headache

2 Dilation of the pupils

3 Dry mouth

4 Sensation that bugs or snakes are crawling on the skin

5 Chest pain

6 Heart palpitations

7 Nausea and vomiting

8 Diarrhea

9 Difficult urination

Also: Profuse sweating; painful rashes, needle marks; infected deep ulcerations; dyskinesia (involuntary twitching of the face, body, and limbs); extreme agitation tremors, loss of coordination, or physical collapse. Injecting amphetamines causes a sudden increase in blood pressure, which can cause high fever, stroke, heart failure, or death.

While effects of oral use of amphetamines may take an hour to become noticeable, smoked or intravenous use of amphetamines—as with methamphetamine—takes effect within five minutes. Different people react differently to methamphetamine. Some are full of energy. Others become anxious or aggressive. Just how aggressive depends on the individual, the environment, and the amount of methamphetamine.

Physical side effects are unpredictable. Even first-time users can suffer traumatic effects, such as panic, vomiting, or seizures, no matter whether they swallow, snort, or inject, although seizures most commonly follow intravenous use. Over time, women may find that their periods become irregular or stop altogether.

Amphetamine users who take large doses of the drug may experience hallucinations, delusions, and paranoia. The paranoia can develop into a psychosis that is extremely difficult to overcome. Organic brain damage associated with paranoid ampheta-mine psychosis can be permanent.

Tolerance to amphetamines, which causes peo-ple to need more and more drug to get the same effect, develops slowly. As tolerance progresses, users often increase the dose to amounts hundreds of times greater than when they started. Many users move from taking amphetamines by mouth to injecting it. As tolerance to the drug develops, rapid heartbeat and feelings of alertness decrease. Mind-changing effects such as hallucinations and delusions become more likely.

Long-term Effects

Long-term amphetamine abuse can make it difficult to swallow, so users often have to force feed themselves. Loss of appetite can cause major vitamin and mineral deficiencies because of poor nutrition. Lack of calcium weakens teeth and bones. Some users experience heart, liver, and lung damage. Continued neglect of a user's health can lead to malnutrition, skin disorders, and ulcers.

Meth abuse also can cause a variety of cardiovascular problems, hyperthermia, and convulsions, all of which can result in death if not treated immediately. But people who use amphetamines for a long time build up such a high tolerance for the drug that even massive doses of amphetamines rarely cause death. Surprisingly, long-term users have reported injecting as much as 15,000 milligrams (a little more than half an ounce) of amphetamines within twenty-four hours without becoming seriously ill.

The sleeplessness that accompanies amphetamine use can eventually lead to a change in brain chemistry and long-term psychological problems. Research shows that as many as half of the dopamine-producing cells in the brain can be damaged after exposure to even low levels of methamphetamine. This brain damage is similar to the damage caused by strokes or Alzheimer's disease. Researchers tested meth addicts who had been off the drug for up to nine months. They found that some brain cells had recovered. However, neuropsychological tests showed that their memory and motor skills had not improved significantly.

People who take large doses of amphetamines over an extended period of time may experience hallucinations, delusions, and paranoia. The paranoia can develop into a psychosis that is extremely hard to overcome.

Amphetamine Psychosis

The term psychosis generally describes a break with reality. People suffering from paranoid psychosis cannot tell the difference between what is real and what is only going on in their head. They may hear things or see things that are not there. They may believe that people on TV are speaking directly to or about them. They may think that strangers are talking about them behind their backs. They may also believe that they are all-powerful and can do anything and everything. Some may completely lose contact with reality and actually act on these delusions. A few commit suicide.

Amphetamine abusers who inject the drug over a long period of time may experience a similar disorder called amphetamine psychosis. An individual suffering from amphetamine psychosis may experience hallucinations and paranoia. Once the drug wears off, there may be fewer hallucinations, and eventually none. But feelings of paranoia can linger, as can increased heart rate and labored breathing.

In 1969, doctors induced psychosis in four healthy male volunteers who had used large amounts of amphetamines in the past. The volunteers were given hourly doses of dextroamphetamine sulfate. At first there were no significant changes, but within twelve hours two of the patients began to show clear-cut signs of psychosis. Within twenty-four hours, the rest of the patients began to show the signs.

At first, the men were high, euphoric. Then they sank into depression and could hardly stand the sight of food. Hospital staff had to convince them to eat. None of the young men slept during the first twenty-four hours, but they were aware of their surroundings and in touch with reality.

Then they became taciturn. They would not discuss their feelings. They asked suspicious questions about noises they heard and items in their room. Soon, their questions turned to paranoia and hallucinations.

Once doctors stopped the amphetamine doses, the participants started talking freely again. Their paranoia lasted for another eight hours. In a 1973 study, some participants continued to suffer

Signs of Amphetamine Abuse

Behaviors:
- false sense of confidence and superiority
- extreme excitement and talkativeness
- bizarre behavior
- aggressiveness and hostility
- restlessness
- nervousness
- irritability and argumentativeness
- depression, anxiety, and moodiness

Physical signs:
- dilated pupils
- dry mouth and nose
- chemical-smelling breath
- frequent lip licking
- excessive activity
- difficulty sitting still
- loss of appetite
- weight loss
- bloodshot eyes from lack of sleep
- open sores or blemishes
- excessive sweating
- a flushed or tense appearance
- rapid or impaired speech

psychotic symptoms for up to six days. One man suffered symptoms off and on for almost a month. These studies showed that large doses of amphetamine can bring on schizophrenia-like symptoms. Even short-term use can cause paranoid amphetamine psychosis.

But no matter how horrific the symptoms of amphetamine psychosis may be, the craving for the drug can still win out.

4 The Legal Scene

SINCE THE 1960s, amphetamines have been a serious concern for lawmakers. Each new ruling gives law enforcement greater powers to stop the production and trafficking of illegal amphetamines.

Amphetamines became illegal except by prescription in 1965. Laws were passed to stop the trade in black market amphetamines, barbiturates, and other psychoactive drugs. As it became hard for users to obtain legally manufactured amphetamines, they turned to home labs to manufacture methamphetamine. The federal government added amendments to the Chemical Diversion and Trafficking Act of 1988 to limit the amount of over-the-counter cold and allergy medicines that contain

SEIZED EQUIPMENT USED TO MANUFACTURE ILLEGAL METHAMPHETAMINE. THIS LAB WAS CAPABLE OF PRODUCING **13,200** POUNDS (**6,000** KILOGRAMS) OF THE DRUG PER WEEK, AT A STREET VALUE OF APPROXIMATELY **$22.8** MILLION.

pseudoephedrine, a key ingredient in methamphetamine. These amendments require registration and record keeping for precursor drugs.

In 1998, Congress passed an amendment to the Higher Education Act that denies loans, grants, and work-study jobs to students with drug convictions.

In a continuing commitment to waging the so-called War on Drugs, legislators in Washington, D.C. have instituted government-sponsored treatment and prevention programs. In May 2001, both houses of Congress introduced the Treatment on Demand Assistance Act. This law would have provided states with the money to get people who voluntarily seek treatment for drug abuse into treatment programs right away. Unfortunately, the bill died without being passed.

State Laws

State governments are actively moving toward requiring treatment for those convicted in drug-related crimes rather than simply locking people in prison, according to the National Conference of State Legislatures. More than a dozen states have passed laws since 2001 to relax mandatory minimum prison sentences and to promote treatment instead. These new laws are giving courts the flexibility to address substance abuse as an underlying problem instead of focusing on drug crime. They also help states make better use of limited funds, since keeping drug offenders in prison is expensive and generally does not solve the problem.

Since 1996, Arizona law has required treatment for certain categories of drug offenders. This saved the state $6.7 million in prison costs in fiscal year 1999, even after taking into account the money spent in providing drug treatment. The court may order people who violate probation to participate in more intense drug treatment, community service, or house arrest, but they will not be put in jail.

California passed a similar law in 2000. An Indiana law makes people charged with delivering a controlled substance eligible for treatment instead of prosecution. It also allows young people to remain in the juvenile justice system instead of being tried as adults.

Many states have instituted drug courts, which are special courts that handle cases involving substance-abusing offenders. Florida passed a law that expands the role of their treatment-based drug courts. The law requires treatment for drug offenders along with any criminal sentence, and enforces treatment programs after release from prison. Washington State allows nonviolent drug offenders to choose between treatment and a prison term. Those who fail in treatment go to prison. Wyoming law provides treatment and prevention programs instead of incarceration. Every state now has drug courts in operation or in

TENNESSEE AGRICULTURE COMMISSIONER KEN GIVENS (LEFT) TALKS WITH GOVERNOR PHIL BREDESEN. GIVENS IS CHAIRMAN OF THE GOVERNOR'S TASK FORCE ON METHAMPHETAMINE ABUSE, WHICH WAS CREATED IN 2004. ON THE FORCE'S INCEPTION, BREDESEN CAUTIONED THAT TENNESSEE'S METH PROBLEM COULD NOT BE SOLVED OVERNIGHT. "IT'S TAKEN A GENERATION TO CREATE THIS PROBLEM. BUT AS A STATE, WE HAVE AN OBLIGATION TO ACT NOW."

planning, and since 1995 the U.S. Justice Department's Drug Courts Program Office has made over six hundred grants totaling more than $125 million for these courts.

Many states are also rethinking mandatory minimum sentences, which many once believed to be a necessary weapon in the war on drugs. Several states have eliminated, or created alternatives to, mandatory sentences. Louisiana did away with mandatory life imprisonment for the distribution of certain controlled substances and allows judges to impose sentences from five to fifty years on a case-by-case basis. The act also allows probation, parole, or suspension of sentence for some nonviolent offenses instead of mandatory imprisonment. North Dakota removed mandatory sentences for first-time drug offenders. Connecticut has done the same.

Another program tests adults for drug use when they are arrested. Judges oversee the supervision and treatment of those who test positive. There is evidence that the court-based model does reduce drug use and crime. For juveniles, a Tacoma, Washington court requires offenders to watch other offenders in court. In this way, young people may recognize their own behavior in the actions of others and see that sanctions are applied fairly and evenly.

At the same time, as states are moving toward treatment for less serious drug offenders, they are

Grundy County, Tennessee, is sometimes called the Meth Capital of the Southeast. The county of 14,000 residents has only nine patrol officers. These include the sheriff and only two deputies who patrol the roads at night. Each of the county's three small towns has one night-shift officer. The criminal investigations unit—one officer—makes its home in a trailer beside the jail in the county seat.

staying tough on drug manufacturers and traffickers, including those who endanger children. In 2002, a number of states passed laws concerning the manufacture of methamphetamine. Delaware created tough penalties for methamphetamine trafficking, Illinois increased the prison time convicted traffickers must serve, and Florida set mandatory minimum terms for drug trafficking offenses.

States are also passing laws to protect innocent bystanders. Kentucky, Minnesota, and Washington have created special provisions regarding minors who are exposed to the harmful toxins of methamphetamine labs. Oklahoma now allows the state to reimburse local law enforcement agencies for the cost of cleaning up illegal drug labs. Kansas, New Mexico, and Colorado now distribute a percentage of money forfeited in drug cases toward prevention and treatment.

Illegal Use of ADD and ADHD Drugs

In order to control possible abuse of ADHD drugs while ensuring that enough is manufactured to supply legitimate needs, the DEA regulates amphetamine prescriptions. The agency, which sets the yearly quotas for how much ADHD medicine can be produced and prescribed, continues to increase those quotas. Between 1993 and 2000 the quota for Adderall increased 3,750 percent. At the same time, because drugs like Adderall and Dexedrine are the most highly addictive of legal drugs, the agency has classified them as Schedule II drugs. Schedule II drugs are subject to strict controls and abuse is subject to severe legal penalties.

Today, ADHD drugs are some of the most commonly stolen prescriptions and are the most often abused of legal prescription drugs. Most abusers are young people, according to the DEA. And most dealers are also young people. Almost 7 percent of high school students had used Ritalin illegally in 1996, according to a 1997 Indiana University study, and some 2.5 percent had used it monthly or more often. Moreover, according to a study in the journal *Psychology in the Schools*, more than a third of students who take attention deficit medication have been asked to sell or give away their drugs. And more than half of students who are not on the medication know students who have sold or given away their pills.

In an effort to decrease abuse of Adderall, Shire Pharmaceuticals, the company that now produces it, developed a longer-acting capsule so that students would not have to take their medicine during the school day. In 2001 the FDA approved Adderall XR as a once-a-day treatment for ADHD.

However, abusers who want Adderall or other amphetamine-based prescription drugs find other ways to obtain it. They may threaten or beat up classmates to get their pills, fake ADHD to get a doctor to write them a prescription, buy the drug from semi-legal pharmacies on the World Wide Web, forge prescriptions, or steal from school offices or pharmacies.

Adults and ADD Drug Abuse

Students are not the only people at schools who abuse these drugs. Several school staff members have been arrested for stealing Ritalin and Adderall from students. In 1998, a special education teacher at a Nashville elementary school was fired after she was caught on videotape stealing ADHD medicine from a secretary's desk. In 2002, a school nurse in Ohio contacted police after noticing that some drugs were missing. Officers set up a surveillance camera that captured pictures of the school janitor stealing students' ADHD drugs.

As a generation of children who take ADHD

During the 2001 school year a teacher in Berks County, Pennsylvania heard that several students were passing drugs around. A fifteen-year-old male student had shared some of his Adderall pills with a group of girls. A doctor prescribed the pills to help the boy concentrate. The girls wanted to get high. The school expelled the girls and police charged them with possession of a narcotic. The boy was also expelled and police charged him with distribution of a narcotic.

drugs grows into adulthood, thefts have moved away from schools and into the community—into the workplace, the military, and even into jails.

Because of the costs—both financial and human—connected with enforcing anti-drug policies, many agencies have started focusing on treatment and prevention programs.

5 Withdrawal and Treatment

THE RISKS OF abusing amphetamines far outweigh any short-term high they may provide. Withdrawal from amphetamines can range from mild discomfort to a life-threatening experience. Treatment can be expensive, and staying clean after treatment is far from guaranteed, but the rewards of living a drug-free life are immeasurable.

Doctors first studied the effects of amphetamine withdrawal in 1972. Fifty users had been on fairly high doses for at least five months and wanted to quit. During their withdrawal, the clinical depression of all of the test subjects increased. Their sleep patterns also changed, with an increased amount of rapid-eye movement (REM) for the first several weeks of withdrawal. REM decreased as their bodies

DR. DEBORAH MASH OF THE UNIVERSITY OF MIAMI SCHOOL OF MEDICINE. BASED ON HER STUDIES OF MORE THAN EIGHTY ADDICTS, DR. MASH SAYS THAT THE PLANT EXTRACT IBOGAINE IS "EXTREMELY EFFECTIVE" IN BLOCKING SYMPTOMS OF WITHDRAWAL FROM AMPHETAMINES AND OTHER DRUGS.

withdrew from amphetamines. Urine tests showed that at first they excreted a high amount of norepinephrine metabolism in the brain. Norepinephrine plays a role in elevating mood and keeping people alert. As withdrawal continued, a smaller amount was released. Suddenly stopping the use of amphetamine can lead to a severe depressive reaction. This reaction is usually temporary, but it is enough to push many users back toward the drug.

Overdose and Emergency Treatment

The toxic dose of amphetamine is different for each individual and depends on how much tolerance they have built up. Blood levels give little information about how severe an overdose is. Emergency room personnel will look primarily at the symptoms. These symptoms include:

- dilated and reactive pupils
- shallow, rapid respiration
- fever
- chills
- sweating
- hyperactive tendon reflexes
- restlessness
- aggressiveness
- anxiety
- confusion
- delirium
- hallucinations

Former meth user Karl Greenfeld described his withdrawal experience in *Time* magazine in 2001:

> *After that first hit of speed, [you become] gloriously, brilliantly, vigorously awake. Your horizon of aspiration expands outward, just as in your mind's eye your capacity for taking effective action to achieve your new, optimistic goals has also grown exponentially. Then, eventually, maybe in an hour, maybe in a day, maybe in a year, you run out of speed. And you crash.*

The sparkle and shine were sucked out of Karl's life. He fell into a depression that was a chemical reaction to the destruction of the dopamine-producing cells in his brain. He had to make a choice—either to continue feeding his addiction, or begin the painful withdrawal process.

- irregular heartbeat
- headache
- hypertension or hypotension
- rapid heartbeat
- circulatory collapse
- syncope (temporary loss of consciousness due to a sudden decline in blood flow to the brain)
- nausea
- vomiting
- diarrhea
- abdominal cramps
- convulsions

Hospital emergency departments often see the effects of amphetamine and methamphetamine abuse. Emergency room personnel treat patients who come into the emergency room with no life-threatening signs by observing them and sometimes offering drugs to sedate them.

For patients with more severe complications, they will make sure there is a clear airway, provide hydration if needed, and provide a calm and soothing environment. Depending on a patient's symptoms, ER workers may pump the stomach, monitor urine output, administer medications for high blood pressure, or give diuretics to reduce fluid in the lungs. Electrolyte and glucose tests are preformed on patients with seizures or unstable mental status.

Antipsychotic medications such as chlorpromazine and haloperidol can help manage agitation and psychosis. Other treatments include ingesting charcoal to absorb an overdose of amphetamines in the stomach, sedatives to control over-stimulation of the central nervous system, and sophisticated drugs to control cardiovascular problems or liver and kidney damage.

Emergency room staff also have to look for common complications of amphetamine and methamphetamine abuse. Because amateur chemists often make methamphetamines in an uncontrolled environment, there is no guarantee of what any individual dose of methamphetamines contains, and there is no way to know the amount of these chemicals in the body. Tests have shown lead, other metals, and organic solvents in the blood of methamphetamine users.

Inpatient Care

Patients who come into the emergency room suffering from amphetamine overdose may be admitted to the hospital for further care. Those with unstable pulse and blood pressure, chest pain, difficulty breathing, fluid in the lungs, seizures, or persistent psychosis may be admitted. Certainly those at risk for stroke or cerebral hemorrhage (bleeding in the brain), or coma will be kept for observation. Those exhibiting psychosis will be referred to the psychiatric ward for treatment.

Inpatient programs are often too short to be affective. People withdrawing from amphetamines are just beginning to function more normally two weeks after they stop using the drug. In many programs, amphetamine users spend only ten to fourteen days as inpatients. They then move to outpatient counseling, which may be less effective. After less than a month, many are back in the situation that led them to abuse amphetamines in the first place.

Long-term Treatment

Abstinence is the only cure for the effects of amphetamine abuse, but there are treatments that can help ease the process of getting clean. Cognitive behavioral therapy can help the former abuser alter behaviors and address underlying problems that led the individual to abuse drugs. Recovery programs teach coping skills and how to manage one's life without drugs. Self-help groups such as Narcotics Anonymous can provide a support group of people going through the same struggle. Educating patients about the dangers of amphetamines is a prominent feature of effective treatment programs.

Treatment Trends

Treatment programs can last from one month to six months and require from one to thirteen hours per week. Some treatment programs emphasize life skills, while others focus on family support or religion. Some programs are more strict than others. Some serve women only or focus on one specific race, but all treatment programs are based on the belief that addiction is a chronic disease.

Holly had been in a treatment program for twenty-one days when she ran away from home. For over a month, she lived in a meth house cluttered with people, drugs, dirty dishes, mold, rats, and cats that peed on piles of clothes that lay everywhere. There was no food and no bathroom door.

"I would be sitting in the living room hearing people scream from the bedroom," Holly told a reporter from The Herald *of Evert, Washington. "I would be watching termites run along the floor, feeling hungry and alone."*

When police finally found her, she was a 75-pound shadow of herself, with black rings around her eyes. Her hands were covered with sores where mites had burrowed under her skin. In court, coming down from her high, Holly's body shook as she listened to a judge order her into a treatment program. She went, but the last thing she wanted was to get clean.

It took about seven days for the physical residue of meth to leave her body. Treatment for methamphetamine is like fixing a broken leg, one counselor said. Patients need a structure that will give their brain chemistry the chance to get back to normal. Just as recovering from a broken leg takes awhile, recovery from methamphetamine takes time.

But Holly's craving for meth did not go away so easily. Two years later, she said: "I love the drug, I absolutely love it. But I never want to go back." Holly coped by staying away from meth and people who use it, and trying not even to think about it. Still, "I will battle this craving until the day I die," she said.

For example, the Matrix Institute on Addictions has had some success with their treatment program, which can last four to six months. It includes at least three group or individual therapy sessions per week. Patients learn about their addiction, how to manage cravings, and how to avoid activities that may trigger a relapse. Matrix also includes family therapy, urine testing, and participation in a twelve-step program.

During withdrawal from amphetamines, users experience intense cravings, which often lead to relapse. Doctors have prescribed the drug fluoxetine to decrease cravings during short-term and imipramine to help patients stick to the program during medium-term treatment.

Drug counselors know that it is difficult for addicts to admit they need help in dealing with an amphetamine problem, so they try to create an environment that is open, welcoming, and accepting. Some demand that their clients be clean when they arrive for treatment, but others do not.

Most treatment is behavioral in nature. This means that rather than using drugs, many treatment centers focus on helping people reshape their behavior. Counselors help patients to understand the temptations that trigger relapse and to create strategies to deal with temptation and relapse. Most treatment programs encourage their clients to join a twelve-step program, such as Alcoholics Anonymous Crystal Meth Anonymous, or Narcotics Anonymous, as a part of their recovery process.

Treatment centers—especially outpatient cen-

Breaking the Addiction

People can break their amphetamine addiction, but it is extremely difficult—both mentally and physically. Joe started taking crystal meth in college to stay awake to study for exams. It should have ended there, but the meth had taken hold. When he could not pay to support his addiction, he stole money from his parents. Sometimes his binges went on for days. His addiction continued for seven years. "I ended up in a straitjacket in a psychiatric ward," Joe told *USA Today*. Joe recovered, but it was not easy. He now works at a drug treatment center in Hawaii, helping others fight their addictions.

ters—recommend twelve-step programs for several reasons. First, this movement has a long history of helping people get clean and stay clean, whatever their drug of choice. Furthermore, many programs do not have the resources to provide support twenty-four hours a day, seven days a week. When cravings hit in the middle of the night, twelve-step programs provide someone to reach out to for support.

Treatment for Amphetamine Psychosis

Researchers have documented dangers for both animal and humans using amphetamines for the first time. And even casual use of amphetamines can precipitate psychotic reactions.

There is not much research to support the treatment of amphetamine psychosis, though a few studies suggest that antipsychotic drugs work. Antipsychotic drugs include the same medications doctors prescribe for patients suffering from schizophrenia, a serious mental illness and thought disorder. This makes sense, because many of the symptoms of schizophrenia are similar to those of amphetamine psychosis. These include delusions, hallucinations, and general lack of desire, motivation, and persistence. Ammonium chloride can help rid the body of amphetamine through the urine. Patients who are extremely agitated and have paranoid delusions and auditory and visual hallucinations respond well to the antipsychotic drugs chlorpromazine and haloperidol. A reassuring, quiet, and non-threatening environment is also helpful in recovery.

The main reason that recovery is such a long and troubled process is that many amphetamine abusers do not want help. They just want to get their hands on more of the drug. And for treatment to really work the user has to want to change.

Once they are in a program, it takes time before users start to feel that they are on the road to recovery. The process is different for each person. After initial treatment, good programs follow their clients for some time to see how well they are doing.

According to the National Institute on Drug Abuse (NIDA), effective treatments for meth addiction involve therapy in which addicts are taught to cope with stress and to have realistic expectations, healthy behaviors, and thinking that is grounded in reality. Recovery support groups also seem to work. A January 2004 National Institutes of Health report suggests that treating meth users with antidepressants may improve their chances of success.

Scientific Research

In order to help people fight amphetamine addiction, treatment centers need to know what works now, not what will work someday. But research takes time.

The Methamphetamine Treatment Project is a research group created to study the treatment of methamphetamine dependence. It began with an

Recovery Takes Time

At fifteen, Jenna did a small line of methamphetamine, and it really freaked her out. She stayed away from the drug for a month and then started using regularly, just for fun. Jenna never noticed how quickly this addiction sneaked up on her. By sixteen, she was using heavily every other day. She lost all respect for herself, and her life began to revolve around the drug.

She attended some Narcotics Anonymous meetings but could not understand what the other people were talking about. What did it mean—"Recovery is in these rooms?" Somehow she missed the part about recovery being a really tough decision that only she could make. Between meetings, she continued her heavy use of methamphetamine, went to school, and stayed awake all night. At one point she had a psychotic episode, and to this day, she still does not know what was real and what was a delusion. At the time she did not care. All she was interested in was consuming as much meth as she could get her hands on.

Jenna lost a lot of weight, had sores all over, and suffered kidney and lung problems. Mentally, she was useless. Still, she kept on using the drug until she was eighteen. That is when she found out her grandmother was dying. It was time for her to make the decision to recover from meth. "I had to be a responsible adult so that I could look myself in the eye," she wrote. When her grandmother died, Jenna was at her side, a mature, drug-free woman.

800-patient randomized study in 2001 to find out which treatment strategies are most effective for meth addiction. They studied the treatment of methamphetamine dependence at a number of different sites with the goal of seeing if the Matrix treatment program could be used effectively in the community drug treatment system.

NIDA set up a program in 2003 to develop different medications to help users fight addiction. In 2004 they were studying ten substances to help addicts recover. Some of these are calcium-channel blockers, drugs usually used to treat high blood pressure; Zofran, which is used to treat nausea; tyrosine, which may increase the production of dopamine in the brain; several antidepressants, which may help relieve the depression that often accompanies withdrawal; and bupropion, an anti-smoking/antidepressant drug.

Other studies may offer hope to those trying to kick a methamphetamine habit. Scientists think that selegiline, which is used to reduce some symptoms of Parkinson's disease, may reverse some of the neurological and cognitive damage that meth use can cause. Vitamin E may help boost natural protective chemicals in the brain. Researchers are also looking for an antidote for methamphetamine overdose, a compound that could leech meth out of the tissues, decrease concentrations of meth, and reduce the high and some adverse effects of the drug.

When It's an Emergency

If a friend has a bad physical reaction to amphetamines, students should call for help. Jillian Cleary was only fifteen the Friday night in February 2004 she tried crystal meth at a slumber party. When she got home, Jillian begged for her mother's forgiveness. "Mom, I'm so sorry. I'm so sorry," she kept saying. "Mom, they talked me into it. I'll never do it again." Jillian never had a chance to keep that promise. She died Sunday afternoon.

Jillian Cleary may not have had to die. Afraid to call for help, her friends had tried to treat her themselves. By the time the sophomore got home, she was very, very sick. By the time she got to the hospital, it was too late. Under the influence of meth, Jillian had inhaled her vomit, which led to the pneumonia that killed her, her father said.

The day after Jillian's death, her mother spoke to the teens in her community. "If a kid gets into trouble, call somebody," she said. "Alert an authority. Tell an adult. Do something. Jill would still be here today if somebody had called 911. If they would have taken her to a hospital, Jill would be alive right now."

Teens Helping Teens

It is important for teens to be able to recognize the signs of amphetamine abuse in family members and friends, since they are the ones most likely to notice changes in those people who are closest to them. Some signs might be a change in attitude toward longtime friends, hanging out with known drug users, losing track of time and missing appointments, lack of reliability, and theft of money from friends and family to pay for drugs.

The teen years are years of big changes, so some of these signs might just be a normal part of growing up. Teens generally are tuned in to their friends and are often the first to know if there is a problem. Friends and classmates are more likely than adults to notice the changes that may be early warning signs of an amphetamine problem. If a young person is concerned about a friend or relative, they should not feel powerless. There are things they can do to help.

How to Help

Teens can help their friends and peers who are abusing amphetamines by helping them to overcome denial and to admit that they have a problem. They can encourage their friends to talk to their parents or another trusted adult, and to continue with treatment or self-help groups.

Talking to a friend about their amphetamine use is not easy. How will the friend react? Will the person get angry and stomp off? Deny the problem?

What to Say

The office of National Drug Control Policy makes the following suggestions about how to approach a friend who may be abusing drugs:

- I don't want anything to happen to you or for you to hurt yourself.
- We all count on you. Your brothers/sisters (if applicable) look up to you/care about you, as do I. What would they do if you were gone? What would I do if you were gone?
- Look at all the things that you would miss out on. Drugs and alcohol can ruin your future and chances to keep your drivers' license, graduate, go to college, and get a job.
- What can I do to help you? I am here to support you.
- Are there other problems you want to talk about?
- Are you feeling pressure to use? Let's talk about it.
- I love you and I won't give up on you.
- If you need professional help or you need an adult to talk to, I can help you find someone. I will be here to help you and support you every step of the way.

Source: National Youth Anti-Drug Media Campaign

Since many teens are uncomfortable bringing up the subject, experts suggest that teens take time to organize their thoughts before they talk. Their tone should be assertive but not aggressive and, at all times, they should stay calm. Being supportive is important.

Some teens start by saying how much they have missed their friend. Others write a note saying they want to talk. No matter how they choose to open the conversation, teens should stick to the facts, describing the changes and behaviors they have noticed, such as taking drugs at a party, blowing off assignments, skipping school, getting into trouble, or just becoming secretive and isolated. Then it is important to listen and really hear what friends are saying. It is also important to keep the lines of communication open, plan a follow-up talk, or decide on a course of action. Sometimes a friend's amphetamine problem is too big for teens to deal with alone. That is the time to talk to a supportive adult.

But remember, spending too much time with friends who abuse drugs can put teens at risk. It is important to keep a balanced perspective, to spend time with friends who do not use drugs, to participate in enjoyable activities, and to keep from dwelling on the situation for too long. It is vital for teens not to let a friend on amphetamines drag them into the downward spiral of drug abuse.

GLOSSARY

adrenaline: A hormone secreted (released) by the adrenal gland. It makes the heart beat increase and can raise blood pressure.

amphetamine: A colorless, volatile liquid used as a central nervous system stimulant.

amphetamine psychosis: A form of psychosis that can result from amphetamine or methamphetamine use, most often occurring after large doses or chronic use.

Attention Deficit Disorder (ADD): A syndrome, usually diagnosed in childhood, characterized by a persistent pattern of impulsiveness, a short attention span, and often hyperactivity, which interferes with academic, occupational, and social performance.

dopamine: A neurotransmitter formed in the brain and essential to the normal functioning of the central nervous system.

drug court: A special court responsible for handling (usually) non-violent cases committed by people who are dependent on illegal drugs.

inpatient treatment: Treatment that requires admission to a hospital or drug treatment facility.

methamphetamine: A derivative of amphetamine used as a central nervous system stimulant both medically and illegally.

neurotransmitter: A chemical substance, such as acetylcholine or dopamine, that transmits nerve impulses across a synapse.

outpatient treatment: Treatment that does not require admission to a hospital or drug treatment facility.

paranoid psychosis: A severe mental disorder, similar to schizophrenia, which is characterized by derangement of personality, loss of contact with reality, and an unfounded or exaggerated distrust of others.

precursor chemical: Chemicals used in the course of legitimate research that can potentially be used in the illicit production of substances such as methamphetamine.

psychoactive drug: A chemical that alters brain function, resulting in temporary changes in perception, mood, or consciousness.

psychosis: A severe mental disorder characterized by derangement of personality and loss of contact with reality.

stimulant: A drug or chemical that temporarily arouses or accelerates physiological or organic activity.

synapse: The junction across which the nerve impulses pass from axon terminal to a neuron.

synthetic: Made artificially by chemical reactions.

tolerance: An adaptation in which exposure to a drug causes changes that result in a reduction in one or more of a drug's effects over time.

FURTHER INFORMATION

Books

Bayer, Linda N. *Amphetamines & Other Uppers.* Philadelphia: Chelsea House Publishers, 1999.

Brecher, Edward M. *Licit and Illicit Drugs; The Consumers Union Report on Narcotics, Stimulants, Depressants, Inhalants, Hallucinogens, and Marijuana—Including Caffeine.* Boston: Little, Brown & Co., 1973.

Cobb, Allan B. *Speed and Your Brain: The Incredibly Disgusting Story.* New York: Rosen Pub. Group, 2003.

Connolly, Sean. *Amphetamines.* Chicago, Ill.: Heinemann Library, 2000.

Hyde, Margaret O. *Drugs 101: An Overview For Teens.* Brookfield, Conn.: Twenty-First Century Books, 2003.

Schleifer, Jay. *Methamphetamine: Speed Kills.* New York: Rosen Publishing Group, 1998.

Wurtzel, Elizabeth. *More, Now, Again: A Memoir of Addiction.* New York: Simon & Schuster, 2002.

Web Sites

Amphetamines.com: The Price of Speed
www.amphetamines.com
This site provides background on the psychomotor stimulants and effects from their use.

Methamphetamine Abuse and Addiction
www.nida.nih.gov/ResearchReports/Methamph/Methamph.html
This site provides information on the dangers of methamphetamine abuse.

National Institute on Drug Abuse
www.drugabuse.gov/DrugPages/Methamphetamine.html
This site provides a list of resources on methamphetamine abuse.

Methamphetamine Fact Sheet
www.whitehousedrugpolicy.gov/drugfact/methamphetamine/index.html
This fact sheet provides an overview of metham-

phetamine abuse, effects, treatment, legislation, and street terms.

Methamphetamine Publications

www.whitehousedrugpolicy.gov/publications/asp/topics.asp?txtTopicID=8&txtSubTopicID=22
A listing of methamphetamine-related publications from various sources.

Where To Get Help

24-hour Alcohol/Drug Help Hotline 1-800-562-1240

Center for Substance Abuse Treatment National Helpline 1-800-662-HELP

Working Drug Free Meth Hotline 1-888-609-METH
www.drug-help.com/meth-help.htm
Or call 1-866-845-8975 to find a treatment center.

Narcotics Anonymous
www.na.org

Al-Anon/Al-Ateen Meeting Locator
www.al-anon-alateen.org/meetings/meeting.html
Or call 1-888-425-2666

Substance Abuse Treatment Facility Locator
findtreatment.samhsa.gov/facilitylocatordoc.htm
A government sponsored treatment facility search page.

INDEX

ABOUT THE AUTHOR

Francha Roffé Menhard was a teacher for more than twenty-five years in both the United States and Japan. She has written advertisements, books, and newspaper columns. Ms. Menhard enjoys traveling, genealogy, and scrapbooking. She lives with her family in the shadow of the Rocky Mountains.